To request permission, contact the publisher at: serenity@elyseburns-hill.com

Paperback ISBN: 9798385951611
This book is part of the Conscious Living with Elyse series.

Published In the United Kingdom of England and Wales by Serenity Publishing,
an Imprint of ElyseBH Consulting Ltd.

Serenity Publishing
ElyseBH Consulting Ltd
Hursley Park Road
Hursley
Hampshire
SO21 2JN

www.elyseburns-hill.com

It Is Safe For Me To Be My best Self

Affirmations and Colouring Book
for Self-Improvement

~ BOOK 1 ~

Elyse Burns-Hill

For Isabelle and Amelia
I work to make the world a better place for you to grow up in.
I love you both so much, you are my everything ♥

Contents

About the Author
Elyse Burns-Hill

I am a single parent of two gorgeous girls (you will notice I dedicated this book to them) and they are my reason for everything I do. I work hard to make the world into a better place by my sharing my learnings about Conscious Living and encouraging others to live the same way.

I am a business leader, currently I am leading a UK accountancy firm as the Managing Director. Again, I aim to lead my teams and guide my clients in a conscious way.

Conscious living became my mission while I was going through the trauma of the breakup from an abusive relationship. I realised that if I wanted to thrive, rather than just survive as I had been for the previous 8 years, I needed to consciously make that happen. That meant that I needed to become conscious about every area of my life. I also needed something good to come out this pain that I was experiencing. As I worked with professionals to help be process the trauma, one common theme that kept coming up again and again, was the idea of doing things consciously. Conscious parenting, conscious leading in business, conscious about the way I lived my life and the relationships I keep. And so **Conscious Living with Elyse** was born.

I write articles and books on Conscious Living. I record videos and podcasts on Conscious Living. And I eat, sleep and breathe Consciously – literally – then I blog about it!

Introduction

Thank you for purchasing this book! I have created it to be the first of a series of books involving colouring (as a quiet, mindful activity for you to do while you recharge) and affirmations so that we can keep reminding ourselves of the importance of conscious behaviours in our day to day lives.

There are 50 affirmations with associated colouring pages in this book. As you colour the page, keep referring to the affirmation on the opposite page; engage with the material, speak it out loud so that you can tell your brain and your body that it is true.

Remember one of the basic principles of brain washing (I promise I'm not trying to brainwash you for any nefarious reasons, but I would like you to brain wash yourself so you can learn to thrive!), when you keep repeating something, eventually it is accepted as truth. Affirmations can be a powerful tool to enhance your thinking and results. It might seem silly to repeat statements that you view as essentially untrue, but give it a try for a month and measure the results for yourself.

Work with the affirmations in a notes app on your phone (or a pocket notebook if you're more of a pencil and paper kind of person) customise them so that you can record yourself speaking your affirmations (use the voice memo app on your phone) and keep listening to it.

You can listen to or read your custom affirmations while you are stuck in line at the shops or waiting for an appointment. Listen to your affirmations every night before you go to sleep and every morning as soon as you wake up – your brain is most receptive at these times, so these times are extra important – give yourself a sneaky extra advantage!

Journal about your successes. Your brain is really good at identifying and remembering all the times real life fails to match with your wishes, so eventually, your brain will expect those failures and will never see anything that doesn't match with those expectations. You need to find a way of remembering all the times things did go right, that match your new positive expectations, in line with the affirmations you are using. Success leads to more success, so keep track!

Forge ahead and give affirmations your best effort for just a month. Affirmations are a simple method to tame your self-talk and use it to your advantage.

My Mind is Focused

My mind is focused.

My mind is clear and calm. I am focused on my priorities.

I live in the present moment. I observe what is going on inside and around me. I concentrate on what is happening now. I let go of past regrets and trying to predict tomorrow. I give my full attention to one thing at a time.

I work and play more efficiently and achieve higher quality results. I become engrossed in savouring my coffee or writing a memo. I write bright ideas and nagging thoughts down, so I can return to them later when my current project is done.

I limit distractions. I turn off my phone during meetings and meals. I spend less time watching TV and browsing online and more time hanging out with family and friends.

I take short and frequent breaks. In between tasks, I take a quick walk or stretch at my desk. I return to my work feeling refreshed.

I care for my body and mind. Adequate sleep, nutritious food, and regular exercise keeps me in top condition.

I meditate and pray. Spiritual activities clarify my purpose. I gain insights into where to focus my attention if I want to lead a meaningful life. I connect with friends who share my goals and encourage me along the path.

Today, I practice managing my attention. Developing my powers of concentration reduces stress and makes me more successful at whatever I do.

Self-Reflection

How can I recover from interruptions at work?

_____
_____
_____
_____

Why is it important to listen attentively?

_____
_____
_____
_____

What is one mental exercise I can do to sharpen my focus?

_____
_____
_____
_____

I Protect Natural Resources

I protect natural resources.

The well-being of the natural environment ensures longevity of the human race. I am committed to protecting natural resources. It is my duty to keep the world I live in safe and healthy.

Recycling allows me to be environmentally responsible. Whenever I use recyclable items, I am conscious about disposing of them properly.

I dedicate some of my time to encouraging others to buy products that are reusable. Leading a recycling drive means making a personal contribution to responsible living. My community is more aware of the benefits because I actively engage them.

I furnish my home with wood pieces made from environmentally sustainable trees. It is important to me to slow down the effects of global warming. My focus is on preserving the world so my children have somewhere healthy and safe to live.

Energy saving initiatives keep my costs down and also preserve resources. When possible I use solar powered equipment.

Although it is costly to convert all my energy needs to solar, I do it in phases. I am happy to be a role model for conscious living.

Today, I am committed to preserving and protecting Earth's natural resources. The likelihood of a better quality of life is more attainable when I conserve. I am proud to be an activist for environmental protection.

Self-Reflection

What approaches can I use to spread the word about environmental consciousness?

_____
_____
_____
_____

In what ways can I be a more responsible user of natural resources?

_____
_____
_____
_____

How do I respond when I see others wasting natural resources?

_____
_____
_____
_____

I Am A Force for Good

I am a force for Good.

I am also a force to be reckoned with. I am totally coming into my power as an amazing human being. I am channelling that force into Good outlets. I am also channelling that force for GOOD… as in forever.

I am consciously choosing to create the best life ever!

I am determined to use all my resources to make the world a better place. My mind comes up with unlimited ideas on solutions that I can implement now. I gather teams of like-minded individuals who also want to be deliberate creators for good on the planet.

I start to work immediately on putting these great ideas into action. I create action plans that are "doable". I have incredible energy to put forth on these projects.

I do what I am best suited for. I use all my skills. I activate my talents.

I delegate everything else to those whose talents are best used in their areas of expertise.

I am proud of my efforts. I am proud of my team.

I am grateful that I have pulled together an amazing team. I am astounded at how everything is coming together perfectly. I am so happy that everyone is doing their best. I am proud that all these projects are moving forward so efficiently. I am proud of my delegation skills.

Today, I am grateful that I have found my purpose. I am proud of my accomplishments so far and know that I am on my perfect path of being a force for Good.

Self-Reflection

What can I do next that will take my projects to the next level?

_____
_____
_____
_____

Who would be perfect to collaborate with on my next projects?

_____
_____
_____
_____

How can I make the greatest impact for good on the planet now?

_____
_____
_____
_____

I Make Progress

I make progress.

I keep moving forward.

I set clear and compelling goals. I give myself something to strive for. My inspiration is strong, and my direction is clear.

I persevere through obstacles. I remember that setbacks are natural. When I hit a roadblock, I find another route. I keep trying, and I learn from each experience.

I embrace change. I keep up with the times. I master new technology and update my skills. I am flexible and optimistic.

I reach out for support. I ask others for help when I need it. I foster collaboration and teamwork. I communicate openly and directly. I share ideas and constructive feedback.

I stay on track. I limit distractions and time drains. I turn the TV on only when there is something specific that I want to watch. I limit the time I spend browsing online or checking for messages.

I evaluate my performance. I keep a journal. Writing about my personal and professional activities helps me to see where I am succeeding and where I want to make positive changes.

I treat myself with kindness and compassion. I adopt lifestyle habits that keep me strong and fit. I validate my feelings and experiences. I take refreshing breaks, so I can relax and restore my energy.

Today, I continue to learn and grow. I stay faithful to myself and my principles. I move closer to fulfilling my dreams.

Self-Reflection

How does perfectionism interfere with progress?

_____
_____
_____
_____

What can I do when I feel like I am stuck?

_____
_____
_____
_____

How can I tell if I am making progress in life?

_____
_____
_____
_____

I Pay Attention to the Details

I pay attention to the details.

I can see the trees in the forest. I can see the ants in the grass. I pay attention to the little details around me. I take notice of the small things that populate my world and make it special.

I know details matter.

Details are important at work and at home. I understand their worth and value.

I am detail oriented. I am proud of the attention I give to small things. I stop and notice them. I am grateful for them. I use my time wisely.

There is power in small things. It is the details that make up the whole. I see how everything connects in this universe. The tiniest speck matters to me.

I concentrate on my surroundings. I see the world in a new light. I notice all the things that make up my life and understand where I can focus to get beneficial results.

Details help me stay on top of the world.

I listen to the small voices. I see the power in paying attention to everything.

Today, I acknowledge the importance of even the tiniest of things. I am grateful for the small things that work together to bring joy to my life.

Self-Reflection

How can I pay attention to details without losing sight of the big picture?

_____
_____
_____
_____

How can I teach my children and others to see and listen to the small things?

_____
_____
_____
_____

What can I do to be more detail-oriented at work?

_____
_____
_____
_____

I Embrace Peace.

I feel calm and comfortable when I welcome peace into my life.

I extend forgiveness. I let go of resentments and disappointments as I remember that I need second chances too.

I practice gratitude. Thinking about my blessings lifts my spirits and gives me energy. I appreciate the kindness of others and experience more harmony in my life.

I face challenges rather than trying to avoid them. I devote my time and energy to figuring out solutions. I replace anxiety with confidence. I show myself that I am capable and strong.

I do one thing at a time. I slow down and give my full attention to my current task. The quality of my work increases, and my activities become more satisfying.

I manage stress. I take breaks during the day, exercise regularly, and think positive.

I monitor my media consumption. I choose to get information from sources that are responsible and constructive. I fill my leisure time with hobbies and socialising rather than watching TV.

I spend time outdoors. Communing with nature awakens my senses and stills my thoughts. I feel part of something larger than myself.

I simplify my life. I shop less and give away possessions that I rarely use. I take control of my schedule, so I can spend more time on my personal priorities. I develop efficient routines and turn off my phone for a few hours each day.

Today, I create more moments of peace for myself and others. I am joyful and serene.

Self-Reflection

Why is it important to make peace of mind a priority?

_____
_____
_____
_____

What is the relationship between peace and patience?

_____
_____
_____
_____

How can I use my breath to calm my thoughts?

_____
_____
_____
_____

I Have the Power and Freedom To Create

I have the power and freedom to create.

Creativity is one of the greatest gifts of all. I make an effort to maximize this gift. I know that the greatest contributions I can make to myself and to the world utilise my creativity.

Everyone has the power to be creative. Yet, many people are afraid to use their creativity. I have the courage necessary to use my creative powers to the fullest.

Creativity requires a measure of boldness and bravery. I have these qualities in abundance. Courageously using my creativity gets easier each day.

I am comfortable putting my unique ideas and creations out into the world. I can handle the opinions of others with ease. I know that most people appreciate my creativity.

I am free to reveal myself to the world. I am confident and secure enough to allow myself to be vulnerable.

I enjoy creating and learning more about myself. Through creativity, I reveal new parts of myself.

Creativity adds to my life tremendously. It allows me to make the greatest impact on the world while simultaneously enriching my own life.

Today, I allow my creative juices to flow. I am open to all the ideas that come into my consciousness. I feel bold and creative. I have the ability to create freely.

Self-Reflection

What potentially great ideas do I have that I am failing to implement?

_____
_____
_____
_____

Why am I resistant to using my creative abilities to their fullest extent?

_____
_____
_____
_____

In what areas of my life would it benefit me to be more creative?

_____
_____
_____
_____

I HAVE THE POWER AND FREEDOM TO CREATE

My Imagination Is An Asset

My imagination is an asset.

I generate new ideas. I reflect on what I have learned so far and where I want to grow. I observe what is going on around me and strike up interesting conversations. I look for connections between seemingly isolated events.

I figure out solutions. I brainstorm about how to overcome challenges. If I test enough approaches, at least one of them is bound to work.

I rehearse my actions. My self-confidence grows as I visualise myself handling situations that used to make me fearful.

There are many things I can do to stimulate my imagination.

I take a long walk or swim laps in the pool. Moving my body encourages my mind to roam.

I invent a story. Creative writing exercises introduce me to new worlds and characters. My life becomes more interesting. I immerse myself in the arts. I find inspiration in paintings, sculptures, and music.

I vary my habits. I change my route for commuting to work or running errands. I work out in the morning instead of taking my usual evening run. Variety supplies more fuel for my imagination.

I play around. Putting on a puppet show with my children helps me to open up and express myself. Pretending to be different characters stretches my perspective.

Today, I use my imagination to broaden my insights and experiences. I dream up new things and put them into action.

Self-Reflection

How does my imagination contribute to my wellbeing and success?

_____
_____
_____
_____

How does sharing my ideas with others activate my creativity?

_____
_____
_____
_____

What is one thing I can do today to nurture my imagination?

_____
_____
_____
_____

My Morning Routines Are Smart

My morning routines are smart.

I start the day feeling happy and energetic. I wake up naturally or get out of bed as soon as the alarm goes off. I avoid using the snooze button.

I drink a glass of water before my coffee. Rehydrating enhances my digestion and makes me more alert.

I stretch my muscles and move around. I go for a run or do some exercises.

I eat a hearty breakfast. I refuel with a balanced meal full of essential nutrients. I whip up a smoothie or an omelette with vegetables.

I plan my day. I review my goals and priorities. I block out time for my most urgent and important activities.

I search for happy news. I spend a few moments reading about medical breakthroughs or watching a story about a school child who raises money for their local food bank.

I give myself enough time to avoid rushing around.

I complete one important task. I write in my journal while my house is quiet. I arrive at the office early to focus on developing social media strategy or analysing complex data.

I treat myself to something special. I play with my children or tend my rose garden. I listen to upbeat music.

Today, I practice morning habits that support my peace of mind and prepare me for success. My cheerful mood carries me through the day.

Self-Reflection

What time do I need to go to bed on weeknights if I want to enjoy pleasant mornings?

_____
_____
_____
_____

What can I do to start getting organised the night before?

_____
_____
_____
_____

How can I make school mornings run more smoothly for my children?

_____
_____
_____
_____

Letting Go Is Joyful

Letting go is joyful.

I make peace with the past. Instead of dwelling on regrets, I am grateful and content with each experience that helps to make me who I am today. I live in the present moment.

I practice forgiveness. When I pardon others, I unburden myself.

I challenge self-limiting beliefs. I review my accomplishments and take on new challenges. I build my confidence.

I accept that some things are outside of my control. I devote my efforts and energy to activities where I can see results. I work on changing myself, rather than losing sleep over what others are doing.

I cut down on possessions. I sort through junk drawers and closets. I give away items I seldom use. I spend less time cleaning and maintaining things. I make my home more spacious and less stressful.

I shorten my to do list. I free up time for having fun and hanging out with family and friends.

I say goodbye to relationships and situations that no longer serve my needs. I seek friends and partners who appreciate me as I am and share my values. I find a new job that allows me to take on more responsibility or enjoy greater balance.

Today, I free myself from attitudes and habits that hold me back. I let go and move on.

Self-Reflection

What is the difference between giving up and letting go?

_____
_____
_____
_____

What is one thing I can do to simplify my life?

_____
_____
_____
_____

Why is quality more important than quantity?

_____
_____
_____
_____

I Appreciate Quiet Moments

I appreciate quiet moments.

I enjoy solitude and stillness.

I pay attention to my thoughts without making judgements. I connect with the divine. I remember my blessings or write a letter to God.

I daydream. I turn my attention inward and indulge my imagination. I increase my self-awareness. I focus on my hopes and dreams. I gain fresh insights and generate new ideas.

I take restorative breaks. I observe nature. I watch squirrels playing and smell cut grass. I stretch my muscles and massage my shoulders. I feel relaxed and energised.

I prepare myself for sleep. I take a warm bath and listen to soft music or falling rain. I sip a cup of chamomile tea.

I go on retreats. I browse online for places to visit or organize my own activities at home.

I work on my hobbies. I paint and sketch. I knit sweaters or assemble jigsaw puzzles. I read novels and science magazines.

I sit in the same room with my partner or a friend. I enjoy their company without having to talk. I feel their presence. We communicate nonverbally.

I disconnect from technology for at least one hour each day. I turn off my phone and computer. I enjoy spending time with myself without distracting images and sounds.

Today, I slow down. I relieve stress and stimulate my creativity by creating more quiet moments in my life.

Self-Reflection

What happens when I listen more and talk less?

_____
_____
_____
_____

What would I do if I scheduled a quiet hour today?

_____
_____
_____
_____

Where can I go when I want some peace and quiet?

_____
_____
_____
_____

I APPRECIATE Quiet Moments

I Am Fully Awake

I am fully awake.

I am vibrant and alive.

I increase my self-knowledge and awareness. I regard myself with honesty and unconditional love. I accept my emotions. I embrace each aspect of myself without making judgements.

I connect with the divine. I open my heart and mind. I recognize our common humanity. I feel like I belong.

I extend compassion to others and myself. I am kind, generous, and helpful. My speech is gentle and encouraging. My actions are intentional and constructive. I listen to others and validate their experiences. I promote healing.

I let go of resentments, regrets, and limiting beliefs. I identify old assumptions that hold me back and replace them with a more empowering attitude. I forgive and move on. I acknowledge my power and take responsibility for my decisions.

I slow down. I focus on one activity at a time. I remember my purpose. I limit distractions. I devote my time and energy to activities that bring me closer to reaching my goals.

I make choices that align with my values. My direction is clear. I stay on track.

I tend to my spiritual needs. I join a faith community or create my own. I read inspirational books and attend retreats. I find role models who inspire me to learn and grow.

I smile and laugh. I enjoy the journey and make friends along the way.

Today, I experience inner peace. I free myself from doubts and fears. I live a full and authentic life.

Self-Reflection

How would I describe my spiritual health?

_____
_____
_____
_____

How do my actions affect others?

_____
_____
_____
_____

Do I feel fully awake? What can I do to feel more alive?

_____
_____
_____
_____

I Plan Ahead

I plan ahead.

Planning helps me figure out where I want to go and what I need to do to reach my destination. I think about my purpose in life and line up my options.

I make deliberate choices that bring me closer to my goals. I set priorities for how I allocate my time and energy. I am willing to change my habits to achieve the things that are important to me.

I prepare for different outcomes. I evaluate the long term consequences of my decisions. If I want to start a family soon, I date others who want children. If I want to travel the world, I choose a profession that allows me to do so.

I learn from experience and adapt to changing circumstances. I prepare for the future while I take care of daily operations.

Planning enhances my financial security. I manage my monthly budget. I save for major milestones like buying a home and sending my children to college.

Planning advances my career. My strategic vision guides me as I weigh job offers. I stay updated on the qualifications needed to succeed in my chosen field or transition to a new industry.

Planning strengthens my relationships. I collaborate with partners who share my passions. I reach out to my friends and family for support. We encourage each other to help make our dreams come true.

Today, I work on my life plan. I chart my course and put my ideas into action.

Self-Reflection

How would I describe my life purpose in one sentence?

_____
_____
_____
_____

What is the difference between planning and worrying?

_____
_____
_____
_____

What are 3 meaningful activities I want to schedule more time for?

_____
_____
_____
_____

Competition Is Healthy

Competition is healthy.

I have little interest in achievements that come to me too easily. Success is more meaningful when I am pushed to achieve it. Competition gives me a chance to prove my worth.

Friendly rivalry in the workplace inspires creativity. When I participate in competition with my co-workers, it is with a light-hearted spirit.

Although I prefer to come out on top, I am conscious that what I do at work benefits the entire team. My focus is on being open to the contribution that puts our business in the best position. I appreciate the talent of those who I work with.

I encourage my kids to participate in sporting competitions at school. It teaches lessons of patience and perseverance at the same time.

Whenever I find myself falling behind my competitors, I choose to be patient instead of getting frustrated. I know that I have what it takes to win, so I dig deep and move forward with composure. Some victories require a calm and deliberate strategy.

When there are others vying for the same accomplishment as me, I am reminded of the importance of staying sharp.

It is unwise to fall asleep on my talent because I know that I am good. I stay aware of my competition and do what is required to sharpen my skills. My abilities are a blessing, so I am committed to making good use of them.

Today, I welcome competition at any level. Victories are sweeter when I stand out amongst my peers and achieve winning results. I know that I have the talent to win.

Self-Reflection

How does it feel to concede victory to a fellow competitor?

_____
_____
_____
_____

How does participating in competition impact my skills in business?

_____
_____
_____
_____

How much does competing with myself push me to surpass past results?

_____
_____
_____
_____

I Love Learning

I love learning.

Knowledge and wisdom are precious. Being a lifelong student enriches my personal and professional life. I sharpen my mind and increase my capabilities. I engage my curiosity. I develop critical thinking skills and make sounder decisions. My sense of accomplishment grows.

I read books. I visit my local library and shop online for fiction and nonfiction titles. I enjoy a wide variety of subjects.

I talk with others. I chat with strangers at the airport and consult with experts in different fields. There is something I can learn from anyone I meet. I listen attentively and ask relevant questions.

I take classes. I attend training sessions at work and complete certification courses online.

I teach what I know. Sharing my knowledge with others introduces me to new ideas and perspectives.

I travel. Touring unfamiliar neighbourhoods and foreign countries expands my horizons. I immerse myself in other cultures. I try out new things and adapt to other lifestyles.

I use technology. I keep up with new developments in tools that help me learn.

I look for lessons in my daily experiences. I study my victories and setbacks so I can enhance my performance.

Today, I seize each opportunity to learn. I seek new knowledge and skills that help me to become more interesting and successful.

Self-Reflection

How does learning help me to adapt to change?

_____
_____
_____
_____

How can I become more teachable?

_____
_____
_____
_____

What is my main motivation for learning?

_____
_____
_____
_____

I Do More and Talk Less

I do more and talk less.

Inspiring trust means more than telling others what I am capable of. It means leading by my actions and allowing others to form their own opinions. I do more and talk less because that is how my true character shows itself.

Loyalty means being committed to people and roles regardless of how difficult things get. I prove my loyalty by supporting a cause without complaining.

When I do things with sincerity and in the interests of others, the intended outcome is achieved. Working on behalf of another person means that my personal interests in that situation take second place.

My friends know that I am trustworthy because I protect their confidence. I have a flawless record of keeping their secrets to myself.

Respecting another person's wishes is the ultimate display of integrity. There are times when I sacrifice myself, but I am okay with that. I know that my true friends always return the favor over and over again.

Sometimes others come to me for advice on how to resolve an issue. Although it is their issue, I sometimes take the step to resolve it myself.

There are times when I am moved to act on behalf of someone else when I sense that they are scared. I am prepared to be the courage that someone needs to make a tough decision.

Today, my actions speak louder than my words. Showing people who I am means leading with the way I do things instead of declaring what my abilities are. It gives me pleasure to extend myself in a meaningful way to those around me.

Self-Reflection

How do I determine when it is okay to just give advice?

_____
_____
_____
_____

Which situations am I most equipped to offer my assistance to?

_____
_____
_____
_____

Which are my most useful skill sets?

_____
_____
_____
_____

I Am A Poised Presenter

I am a poised presenter.

I am happy that I have taken the time to study presenting and leadership. I am proud of myself for how far I have come as a presenter.

I am grateful for all the classes I have taken in body language. I am grateful for all I have learned about leadership. I am applying everything I have learned in order to become a poised presenter.

I am thankful for all the knowledge I have acquired thus far concerning how to have composure in all circumstances. I am grateful for my teachers and mentors who have helped me with my presentation skills.

I am grateful for my speaking coaches. I am thankful for all the courses I have taken over the years. I am blessed to have read many books on how to write and present a speech.

I realize that I gain confidence the more times I present. I am learning new skills about how to present online. I am learning how to do podcasts. I am practicing by doing them frequently.

I am learning how to write better presentations. I am learning how to use technology to my advantage. I am growing in my experience. I am becoming more poised and self-assured.

I do a lot of research on how to become a master presenter. I study vast materials on this topic. I feel prepared. I am poised.

Today, I feel ready and able to make effective, enjoyable, and knowledgeable presentations, whether in person or online.

Self-Reflection

What would make me a more poised presenter?

_____
_____
_____
_____

Who would be a great coach for refining my presentation skills?

_____
_____
_____
_____

Who do I know that could take my presentation skills to the next level and would be willing to be my presentation mentor?

_____
_____
_____
_____

i AM A Poised Presenter

It Is Safe for me to be My Best Self

It is safe for me to be my best self.

I am destined to become my best self. Becoming the best version of myself is my purpose. I am free of fear and hesitation.

It is natural for me to learn, grow, and develop into my ideal self. I am comfortable with what I am becoming.

I am free to become my best self. I recognize that the only obstacle to my development is me. I am getting out of my own way and allowing my best qualities to shine through.

Everyone benefits when I am at my best.

While I am greatly benefiting from this journey, others benefit as well. My family, friends, team, and even the casual acquaintances in my life are better off when I become a better version of myself.

I am kinder, happier, and more generous to myself and others when I show my best qualities.

I am free from the criticism of others. There may be a few people that try to stand in my way as I am evolving into my best self. It is easy for me to ignore these people. I am comfortable with who I am and who I am becoming.

Today, I am better in every way. I feel safe while I take a giant step forward in my personal development. I am choosing to be more today than I was yesterday. I am evolving in a positive direction.

Self-Reflection

Who do I want to become? What characteristics and habits do I have as my ideal self?

_____
_____
_____
_____

What is preventing me from becoming the person I most want to be? What do I believe is in my way?

_____
_____
_____
_____

What can I do today to take one step toward becoming the person I want to be?

_____
_____
_____
_____

I Choose My Actions Intelligently and Carefully

I choose my actions intelligently and carefully.

I make effective decisions because I know what I want to accomplish. My actions are based on the things I want to achieve in my life. By having clear goals, I am able to make decisions that support the achievement of those goals.

A decision that brings me closer to accomplishing my goals is always an intelligent decision.

I know that it is easier to avoid a mistake than to correct one. Therefore, I choose my actions carefully and thoughtfully.

I consider the potential long-term consequences of my actions before I make a final decision. Considering the long-term effects of a decision is intelligent. I am an intelligent person that makes great decisions.

I consider my values before making any decision. Decisions that are counter to my values are later regretted.

It is important that I make choices that are in line with my highest values. I make decisions that increase my self-respect. I avoid making decisions that I later regret. I choose to live according to my beliefs and values and make my decisions accordingly.

Today, I am determined to only make wise decisions. I consider my goals and values before choosing a course of action. I am making progress today through choosing my actions intelligently and carefully.

Self-Reflection

What are the biggest mistakes I have made? What impact did those poor decisions have on my life? Why did I make those decisions?

_____
_____
_____
_____

What is the biggest decision facing me right now? What is the smartest choice I can make?

_____
_____
_____

If I made my decisions more intelligently and carefully, what would the impact be on my life?

_____
_____
_____
_____

I Choose My Actions Intelligently And Carefully

I Speak Up

I speak up.

I have valuable things to say. I speak up with kindness and confidence.

I share my thoughts and feelings. I engage in meaningful discussions. I allow others to get to know me. I strengthen my relationships.

I contribute my wisdom and perspective. Collaborating creates superior solutions because each of us has unique ideas and experiences.

I offer praise and encouragement. I let others know that I notice their progress and appreciate their efforts. I thank them for their feedback and tell them how their advice has helped me to move forward.

I think before I speak. I examine my purpose. I want my words to be kind, honest, and helpful. I make my message as concise as possible so that others will listen to me and know that I respect their time.

I ask for what I want. I remind myself of my worth. I set boundaries. I fulfill my needs while respecting the welfare of others.

I strike up conversations. I practice my small talk. I put down my phone so I can talk with others face to face. Routine errands become more interesting and pleasant when I chat with salespeople and taxi drivers.

I promote harmony. My words honour the truth, resolve conflicts, and draw others closer to me.

Today, I summon up the courage to speak my mind. My voice helps me to express myself and connect with others.

Self-Reflection

What is one thing I would regret leaving unsaid?

_____
_____
_____
_____

Where can I practice my public speaking skills?

_____
_____
_____
_____

How do my childhood experiences affect my willingness to speak up?

_____
_____
_____
_____

I Am Building My Future One Day At A Time

I am building my future one day at a time.

I start each day with the intention of building a brighter future. I know that each day is an opportunity to lift my life to a higher level

I make the most of each day by choosing my actions carefully. I recognise that everything I think and do affects my future. Each thought or action can either help bring me the future I want, or it can make that future further away.

I have a clear vision for my future. I have a plan for creating my ideal future one step at a time, and I am following it as closely as I can. My focus is on doing what I can do today to create the future I desire.

I have big plans, and I know that big plans take time.

I am patient, but I am also optimistic. I feel a high degree of certainty that my ideal future is coming to fruition. I am putting in the work and patiently waiting for the results.

I avoid allowing a day to go by without taking active steps to guarantee my future.

Today, I am more focused than ever on my future. I am making the most of this day and accomplishing as much as I can. My decisions are based on my goals. I am building my future one day at a time.

Self-Reflection

What is my vision for the future? Is it appealing, motivating, and precise? How can I make it even better?

_____
_____
_____
_____

What steps am I taking each day to make that vision a reality? What else could I be doing?

_____
_____
_____
_____

What do I need to remove from my life to improve the odds of being successful?

_____
_____
_____
_____

I Am Building MY FUTURE One Day At a Time

Authenticity Defines My Character

Authenticity defines my character.

In a world full of masks and imitation, I celebrate my true identity. I am proud to share it with others. It is the formula for constantly being at peace with my reality.

My life today represents my unique journey. I embrace each part of my story with pride. I am ready to tell the truth about my life to anyone who asks. There is always a part of my story that has the potential to positively influence someone else.

Being a people pleaser brings more sadness than joy. Whenever my actions or words are inauthentic, I feel unsettled in my soul.

My sense of purpose is important to me. It comes from my own mission as opposed to the motive of others. I refuse to let anyone tell me how to be. My worth is based on how I view myself and the depth of my potential.

When someone meets me for the first time, I show them who I really am. It makes little difference whether they like what they see or hear.

The sound of my voice and the face of my actions represent what I hold firm. Popularity holds little value to me. I prefer to be popular for being true to myself. When I base my actions on positive virtues, I automatically attract positive energy.

Today, when I look in the mirror, I see someone who is proud of their reflection. It is my view of myself that matters most. I dwell at peace in my identity because it is what makes me uniquely me.

Self-Reflection

Where do the greatest pressures to impress usually come from?

_____
_____
_____
_____

How do I ensure that I stay true to myself?

_____
_____
_____
_____

What three things best define my authentic character?

_____
_____
_____
_____

Daily Practice Is Powerful

Daily practice is powerful.

I learn through repetition. I reinforce positive habits and expand my skills. I set goals and work hard. I persevere through obstacles and evaluate my progress.

I nourish my spiritual wellbeing. I reflect and pray each day. I read inspiring texts. I build a community of friends who help me to explore my beliefs and apply them to my life.

I strengthen my relationships. I communicate tactfully and honestly. I resolve conflict respectfully and promptly. I treat others with kindness and respect. I demonstrate compassion for myself, too. Each time I interact with anyone is more practice for these skills.

I strengthen my health each day. I eat healthy. I focus on natural whole foods rich in nutrients and fibre. I start my day with a hearty breakfast. I drink water instead of sugary beverages. I also exercise consistently. I develop my strength and cardio fitness. I increase my balance and flexibility.

I work on my hobbies. Daily practice increases my skills and allows me to complete projects. I learn to play the flute or build a wooden boat. I take cooking classes or join community organizations where I can collaborate with experienced gardeners or long-distance runners.

I advance my career. I take certification courses online and apply my lessons to my daily tasks. I shadow employees who I admire, so I can observe their methods and adapt them to my own strengths.

Today, I am diligent and committed. I enhance my performance through deliberate practice.

Self-Reflection

How can I adopt a growth mindset?

_____
_____
_____
_____

What role does natural talent or hard work play in my ability to reach my goals?

_____
_____
_____
_____

What are my peak hours for learning new information and completing challenging tasks?

_____
_____
_____
_____

Daily Practice is Powerful

I Start Fresh

I start fresh.

Each day is a new beginning. I let go of the past. I appreciate who I am now. I focus on the things I can control and move forward. I forgive myself and others.

I try new things. I learn how to knit a sweater or play pickleball. I experiment with different recipes. I take the scenic route to work.

I adopt healthy habits. I eat eggs and fruit for breakfast instead of sugary cereal. I go to bed early rather than binge-watching TV for hours.

I build my connections and increase my sense of belonging. I deepen my relationships with family and friends. I reveal my inner thoughts and feelings. I introduce myself to a neighbour or another member at my gym. My community grows bigger and stronger.

I revise my schedule. I shorten my to-do list. I cross out activities that drain my energy. I devote my time to my top priorities.

I clear away clutter. I throw away items I no longer use or give them to charity. Getting organised reduces stress and helps me to think more clearly.

I update my goals. I create new challenges for myself. I decide what I want to achieve. I give my life more meaning and direction.

I think positive and take risks. I believe in myself and my abilities. I move beyond my comfort zone. I learn from each experience.

Today, I reinvent myself. I discover my passions and strengths. I feel excited and inspired.

Self-Reflection

What is one thing I need to forgive myself for?

_____
_____
_____
_____

If I wanted to change careers, what new field would I choose?

_____
_____
_____
_____

What are some signs that I need to make a fresh start?

_____
_____
_____
_____

I Do My Part

I do my part.

I make a positive contribution to the world. I am committed to doing my part. I understand my strengths and skills. I leverage my areas of expertise. I focus on doing what comes naturally to me so I can accomplish more.

I take responsibility for my choices. I hold myself accountable for using my resources wisely and reaching my goals.

I set a good example. I ask myself whether my actions align with my values. I manage my emotions and treat others with respect. I try to spread a cheerful attitude. I want my behaviour to be something that others can copy.

I offer practical assistance to others. I watch out for my neighbour's safety and lend a hand when co-workers are overburdened. I provide moral support and encouragement. I offer empathy and compassion when I see someone struggling. I wish others well and rejoice in their victories.

I exceed expectations at my job. I challenge myself to make innovations and deliver superior results.

I build strong and mutually beneficial relationships. I engage in honest, tactful, and positive two-way communication.

I raise my children to be kind and responsible. I teach them to value work and persevere through obstacles.

Today, I take action and strive to be highly effective. I have important and unique gifts to share with those around me. Doing my part helps me to live up to my potential and create a meaningful legacy.

Self-Reflection

What would happen if I failed to do my share of chores around the house?

_____
_____
_____
_____

How can I play a more effective role in team projects at work?

_____
_____
_____
_____

How do I define doing my fair share in my community?

_____
_____
_____
_____

I Hear My Greater Calling

I hear my greater calling.

I hear my greater calling and I must respond. It is overwhelming. But in a good way.

I feel like the Phoenix, like my smaller self is being burnt into ash in order for my greater self to be born from the ashes.

I realize that it is time to get busy with my greater calling. I rise triumphant as the New Me emerges from the flames of the past.

I avoid trying to ignore the great voice within. It overcomes me. It becomes me. My new me is awakening like the dawn.

I allow my small self to transform into something greater. Something more powerful. Someone who I am surprised to see is the true me.

I accept and receive my new calling!

As I allow this greater Me to be born, I accept the challenge. I take up my new calling. I seize the day. I rise up with newfound strength and courage. I feel like I am on fire with an eternal flame.

Today, I accept that I am greater than I could have ever imagined. I expand into this new powerful phoenix. I spread my wings and fly.

Self-Reflection

What do I need to let go of in order for my greatest calling to come forth?

_____
_____
_____
_____

How can I release the Small Me, in order for my Greatest Me to show up?

_____
_____
_____
_____

How can I listen deeper to my greatest self?

_____
_____
_____
_____

I Complete What I Start

I complete what I start.

When I start a project, I see it through to the end. My success depends on being persistent and thorough.

I consider my priorities before I take on a new project. I focus on activities that are meaningful to me. I pursue work that is aligned with my goals. Prioritizing helps me to use my resources wisely. I persevere because I care about what I am doing.

My confidence grows when I cross the finish line. I create a record of achievements that I can build on. I see how I contribute to making my world a better place.

I develop habits that help me to keep complicated projects on track and give myself incentives along the way.

I break tasks down into smaller steps. I set intermediate deadlines. If I want to buy a house by the end of the year, I calculate how much money I need to save each month.

I take breaks along the way. Downtime clears my mind, and restores my enthusiasm. I return to work with more energy.

I let go of unrealistic expectations. I know that perfectionism can make me anxious and hold me back. Instead, I focus on doing a good job with the time and budget I have available. I find fulfillment in living up to my potential.

Today, I follow through on what I start. I commit myself to overcoming any barriers.

Self-Reflection

What is one incomplete project I want to finish?

_____
_____
_____
_____

How would adjusting my goals help me to see things through?

_____
_____
_____
_____

How do I feel when I persevere through distractions and challenges?

_____
_____
_____
_____

I Keep My Promises

I keep my promises.

My ability to maintain the trust of others is important to me. There are various ways to gain people's trust, and keeping promises is one of them.

Fulfilling promises indicates that I am a reliable friend, co-worker, and family member. I like when the important people in my life feel like they can count on me.

Before making promises, I ensure that following through is a realistic expectation. The last thing I want is to be frivolous with promises and end up disappointing others. I accept that, like everyone else, I have limited capabilities.

My children look to me for making their wildest desires come true. At times, I am tempted to make deals with them to get them to behave. But I avoid doing that.

I know that making unfulfilled promises to children causes them to distrust me. It is vital that they know I am reliable. There are cases when it is imperative that I deliver what is required. Keeping that in mind helps me to always be honest with them.

When situations occur beyond my control, I am quick to apologise for unfulfilled promises. It is important that others understand that my intention is sincere.

Today, I vow to live by honest standards and keep expectations realistic. I love to make other people's desires reality. But I commit to being honest with myself and them about what I able to do for them.

Self-Reflection

How do I feel when other people break their promises to me?

_____
_____
_____
_____

How different is a promise from an assurance?

_____
_____
_____
_____

What are some of the strategies I can use to deliver disappointing news to others?

_____
_____
_____
_____

I Distance Myself From Negativity

I distance myself from negativity.

I am a peacekeeper. Relationships are more durable when they are fuelled by positive energy. I keep away from negativity as a way to maintain amicability.

Tensions are difficult to handle, so I prefer to diffuse them early. My home is a peaceful place because of that. I set a tone of positivity by how I deal with issues. Instead of pointing the finger, I focus on finding resolutions.

This approach keeps issues from blowing up unnecessarily. I appreciate when my family members come to me for assistance to resolve something.

When a friend is dealing with a personal issue, I am careful with giving advice. It is important to encourage open-mindedness and forgiveness. Doing this sets the tone for my friend to deal with the situation maturely.

Although I only hold responsibility for my own actions, I look out for my friends. I do what I am able to lift them out of negativity.

Personal conflict impacts emotions and makes it difficult to think clearly. Before my own relationships get to the point of conflict, I choose to wave the white flag. Promoting peace is hardly an admission of guilt. It is a sign of willingness to forgive and forget.

The further away from negative energy I am, the greater my quality of life.

Today, each of my days is rich because of the soul-filling energy that I promote. I know that I am responsible for creating the life that I am happy with. That starts by focusing on positive living.

Self-Reflection

What are some of the consistently negative influences in my life?

_____

_____

_____

_____

How do I tell someone that their approach is harmful without hurting their feelings?

_____

_____

_____

_____

What steps do I take to diffuse a situation that is already in a state of negativity?

_____

_____

_____

_____

I Distance Myself from NEGATIVITY

My Concentration Is Strong

My concentration is strong.

I train my mind to focus.

I limit multitasking. I give my full attention to one activity at a time. Taking a mindful approach helps me to work more productively and experience less tension. I accomplish more in less time.

I create a daily meditation practice. I sit down for a few minutes each day to still my mind and observe my thoughts. As I practice, I learn how to choose the objects of my attention in any situation.

I take care of my mind and body. My physical and mental wellbeing are closely connected. I prioritize sleep, good nutrition, and staying active. I exercise my mind with games that sharpen my mental abilities.

I deal with stress constructively. It is easier to concentrate when I feel relaxed.

I pause for breaks throughout the day. A brief walk or a chat with a friend refreshes me. I return to work with greater enthusiasm and a sharper focus.

I minimise distractions as much as possible. I put aside worries and doubts. I clear away physical clutter. I turn off electronic devices and try to find a quiet place to work. When I am interrupted, I bounce back quickly. Instead of becoming irritated, I accept diversions as a natural part of life.

Today, I remind myself to focus on the present moment. My mind is calm and clear. I am able to concentrate more fully for longer periods of time.

Self-Reflection

How does paying attention to my surroundings help me to lead a more fulfilling life?

_____
_____
_____
_____

How does technology affect my ability to concentrate?

_____
_____
_____
_____

What is one thing I can do to help lengthen my attention span?

_____
_____
_____
_____

I Give Myself Room To Grow

I give myself room to grow.

I am a work in progress. I give myself room to learn and grow.

I try new things. I keep an open mind and move beyond my comfort zone. I go skydiving or write poetry. I listen to country music instead of opera. I replace my usual morning run with a calisthenics session.

I seek out challenges. I volunteer for difficult assignments at work. I talk about sensitive subjects with my family and friends.

I ask questions. I gratify my curiosity. I consult experts and small children.

I welcome feedback. I invite colleagues and clients to let me know what they think about my performance. I thank my loved ones for helpful reminders to pick up after myself or talk more slowly. I use their input to make positive changes.

I teach others. I tutor high school students and mentor newcomers in my field. I show my grandparents how to play video games.

I read books. I explore nonfiction titles and great literature. I study science and history.

I take classes. I sign up for adult education courses at my local university and subscribe to e-learning platforms.

I make learning fun. I visit my local library to browse for free audiobooks, movies, and events. I travel to another country or around my neighbourhood. I practice speaking foreign languages at ethnic restaurants and grocery stores.

Today, I train my mind to think. I add to my knowledge and skills. I pursue my passion for learning.

Self-Reflection

What is one new skill that would help me to advance my career?

_____

_____

_____

_____

What is the difference between working hard and working smart?

_____

_____

_____

_____

Why is it important to adopt a growth mindset?

_____

_____

_____

_____

I Build Strength

I build strength.

I strengthen my body and mind. I increase my power and develop new capabilities.

I eat nutritious foods. I fuel up on balanced meals and wholesome snacks. I eat plenty of vegetables and fruits, and cut back on empty calories.

I work out. I lift weights or take a yoga class. I train for strength, flexibility, and balance. I manage my weight and keep my heart healthy.

I give myself adequate rest and sleep. I go to bed and wake up on a consistent schedule. I take occasional breaks throughout the day to stretch my limbs and refresh my thoughts.

I manage stress. I find constructive ways to deal with noisy neighbours or traffic jams. I listen to music, take a warm bath, or stroll through the park. I resolve conflicts by respecting the needs of others as well as my own.

I continue learning. I gain knowledge and insights through reading and traveling. I ask questions and engage in deep conversations.

I think positive. I focus on what I have to gain. I remember to be grateful for the good things in my life.

I connect with others. I surround myself with family and friends who give me valuable feedback and support.

I practice my faith. My spiritual beliefs give me inspiration, comfort, and strength.

Today, I flex my mental and physical muscles. I am willing to push myself so that I can achieve more. Being strong enables me to perform at my peak and reach my potential.

Self-Reflection

How can challenges and setbacks help me to become stronger?

_____
_____
_____
_____

2. Why is it important to tolerate discomfort sometimes?

_____
_____
_____
_____

3. What is the relationship between self-acceptance and strength?

_____
_____
_____
_____

My Life Is Always Moving Forward

My life is always moving forward.

My life is sometimes moving forward slowly. Usually, my life is moving forward quickly. However, my life is always moving forward.

I am a big believer in making progress each day.

Even one small step can make a difference. I only need to lay one good brick each day to eventually build a huge wall.

I am always laying more bricks in the wall of my life. Each brick matters. I lay these bricks as quickly as I can, but I can be satisfied with a single brick.

I am committed, but I am also patient when necessary.

I am very clear on the direction of my life. I know where I want to go. I am focused on moving my life in that direction.

My visions of the life I want to live pull me forward each and every day. My decisions support the vision I have for my life. My actions take me one step closer to my ideal life.

My life is always moving forward. One step at a time. One day at a time. I am getting closer each day.

Today, I am moving my life forward in a big way. Today, I am taking big steps and creating big results. I am making rapid progress today.

Self-Reflection

What is my vision for my life? Are my plans big enough? Are they worthy of me?

_____
_____
_____
_____

What can I do today, tomorrow, and next week that will ensure that my life is moving forward?

_____
_____
_____
_____

How can I get to where I want to go faster? Why have I been moving slower than that so far?

_____
_____
_____
_____

I Balance Body and Mind

I balance body and mind.

My physical and mental wellbeing are closely related.

I stay active. Physical exercise lifts my spirits and clarifies my thinking. I burn calories, strengthen my heart, and tone my muscles. Visiting the gym or running through the park helps me to lead a fuller life.

I eat a healthy diet. I nourish my body and mind with delicious whole foods. I enjoy 5 or more servings of vegetables and fruits each day. I cut back on added sugar and salt.

I sleep well. I go to bed and wake up on the same schedule each day. I wake up feeling energized and refreshed.

I deal with stress constructively. I practice yoga and deep breathing. I take a bath and listen to soft music.

I develop mutually supportive relationships. I spend time with family and friends. I discuss my thoughts and feelings. I ask for help when I am struggling.

I think positive. I look on the bright side when I run into difficult situations. I forgive myself and others for past disappointments. I use my self-talk to build my confidence and motivation.

I laugh and play. I watch funny movies and cat videos. I share jokes with my friends. I sing karaoke and dance with brooms.

I tend to my spiritual wellness. I meditate and pray. I live according to my faith.

Today, I recognise the connection between my body and mind. I make choices that keep me strong and fit.

Self-Reflection

How do my emotions affect my health?

_____
_____
_____
_____

How can I increase my self-awareness?

_____
_____
_____
_____

What is my body saying to me now?

_____
_____
_____
_____

I Clear My Mind

I clear my mind. I am free of disturbing thoughts.

I forgive others and myself. I say goodbye to grudges and resentments. I give myself credit for trying. I value learning from experience.

I challenge assumptions that hold me back. I use positive language. I take responsibility for my choices. I remember my achievements and trust my abilities. I conquer my doubts.

I open myself up to new opportunities. I take worthwhile risks and try different things. I increase my knowledge and skills.

I focus on the things I can control. I accept uncertainty. I devote my time and energy to projects that align with my values and add meaning to my life. I grow closer to reaching my goals.

I move around. Physical activity helps me to think more clearly. I run through the park or ride my bike. I pull weeds in my garden and mop my kitchen floor.

I keep a journal. I express my thoughts and feelings. I write about my daily experiences or draw pictures.

I seek support. I turn to my family and friends for encouragement and constructive feedback. I feel loved and cared for.

I take refreshing breaks. I relax my muscles and take deep breaths. I visualize myself making positive changes. I cultivate gratitude.

Today, I feel peaceful and content. My mind is like a clear sky after the wind has blown the storm clouds away. I greet the day with confidence and hope.

Self-Reflection

What is one piece of old baggage I am ready to get rid of?

_____
_____
_____
_____

How does taking action help me to stop worrying?

_____
_____
_____
_____

How do I define peace of mind?

_____
_____
_____
_____

I Wait Patiently

I wait patiently.

I have the wisdom and strength to be patient. Staying calm makes me happier and healthier.

I focus on the long term. I keep minor irritations in perspective. I think things through instead of acting on impulse.

I use down time productively. I read a magazine or check my email while standing in line at the grocery store. I proofread documents for work while I sit in the waiting room at my doctor's office. I shop for gifts or return phone calls when my flight is delayed.

I take care of myself. I am able to bear annoyances more successfully when I avoid becoming hungry, thirsty or sleepy.

I listen to my children. I let them learn and grow at their own pace instead of trying to force my own schedule. I stay calm even when they are acting out. I make lists and plan ahead, so outings and errands run more smoothly.

I deal constructively with pressure at work. I treat my team with respect even when we disagree. I give others an opportunity to learn even when I could complete the task faster myself.

I give new activities time to show results. I stick to a diet or workout routine for a few months instead of jumping from one fad to the next. I complete a training course rather than giving up after the first tough class.

Today, I tolerate difficult situations with humour and ease. I am patient with others and myself.

Self-Reflection

What happens to my body when I become impatient?

_____
_____
_____
_____

What is the difference between patience and passivity?

_____
_____
_____
_____

How does patience affect my daily commute?

_____
_____
_____
_____

I Am Drawn to Positive People and Situations

I am drawn to positive people and situations.

I am attracted to positive people and avoid those who are negative. The company I choose to keep has a big impact on my attitude, happiness, and success. The people in my life influence my life, so I choose them very carefully.

I have high standards for the people in my life. I am generous and kind, but I have limits. I remove those people from my life that are negative or require too much of my attention and energy. I am drawn to those who can add something positive to my life.

I avoid negative situations. Before I become involved in any situation, or with any person, I consider the impact it will have on my life. Those situations and people that have a positive impact on my life are appealing to me. I can easily avoid negative situations and people.

Some people are drawn to drama. I avoid drama. I appreciate simple, positive experiences. My life is more enjoyable this way. I accomplish more this way.

Today, I am focused on positive people and situations. I am attracted to people and situations that enhance my life. I am a magnet for all the positive things that the world has to offer.

Self-Reflection

Who is the most negative person in my life? Why am I permitting them to remain in my life? What can I do to make my experience with this person more positive in the future?

_____
_____
_____
_____

What is the most negative situation in my life? What can I do to make it better?

_____
_____
_____
_____

How would my life change if I avoided negative people and situations?

_____
_____
_____
_____

I AM DRAWN TO POSITIVE PEOPLE AND Situations

Empathy Builds Humility

Empathy builds humility.

I stand in solidarity with my brothers and sisters around me. Understanding their realities educates me on how to stand in defense of their causes.

When I actively listen to the plight of others, I gain a greater sense of the challenges that they face. I sincerely connect with their feelings by putting myself in their shoes. The way forward is much clearer to me when I do that.

I am able to lend a hand to someone who I love by carefully understanding their situation. My support is rooted in common knowledge and connected emotions.

The difficulties that my friends face feel more personal to me when I take the time to connect with them emotionally. I am reminded that even when I feel like things are tough, there is always someone who is having a tougher time.

Shifting perspectives challenges what I am conditioned to think. It allows me to come face to face with my own privilege and practice humility.

Thinking about what someone else is going through takes me away from focusing on myself. Although I have my own challenges, it is important to think wider than my own reality. I learn valuable life lessons by embracing others in their difficult times.

When I tell someone that I understand how they feel, I say it with meaning. That meaning comes from stepping out of my shoes and into theirs.

Today, I embrace the role of being my brother and sister's keeper. There is more meaning to life when I focus more on those around me that I do on myself.

Self-Reflection

How often do I practice empathy?

_____
_____
_____
_____

How often do I call on my loved ones when I feel like being listened to?

_____
_____
_____
_____

What does empathy look like when someone experiences tragedy?

_____
_____
_____
_____

I Tap Into the Magic of Nature

I tap into the magic of nature.

I am thankful for nature and the gifts that it brings to me. I realise just spending 5 minutes in nature truly enjoying its beauty helps me find beauty in all things and all people.

I am grateful for the peace that nature brings me. I can just look out my window and enjoy the light through the trees and it brings forth a breath of calm in me. I am glad that I live in a place surrounded by nature.

I am grateful for the rain. I know that I get negative ions from the rain, which puts me in a good mood.

I am grateful for the rainbow after the rain, which restores my hope in the world. I am grateful for the sun that shines each day.

I am grateful for the opportunity to walk barefoot in the grass and for the times I have been able to go to the beach and wiggle my toes in the sand. I am grateful for the peace that ocean waves bring.

I am grateful for the times I have been able to hike in nature. I love to catch nature doing amazing things. I love to see wildlife from safe distances. I love noticing the little things, like finches taking a bath in a bowl of fresh rainwater.

As I immerse myself in nature, my eyes catch all manner of magical things. I notice the ladybird crawling on my wall. I catch glimpses of a squirrel leaping from tree to tree. I notice the diligent hard-working ants.

Today, I learn so much from nature. I am filled with abundant gratitude for its lessons and the peace and happiness that it brings into my life.

Self-Reflection

What can I do to tap into nature more?

_____
_____
_____
_____

How can I be a better caretaker of nature?

_____
_____
_____
_____

How can I share the bliss of nature with others?

_____
_____
_____
_____

I Bring My Dreams To Life

I bring my dreams to life.

My life is joyful and rewarding.

I dare to dream big. I take worthwhile risks and maximise my opportunities. I look for places where I can add value and make a difference.

I limit distractions. I am selective about watching TV and browsing online. I simplify my lifestyle by clearing away clutter and cutting down on possessions. I free up more time and energy to devote to my passion projects.

I live according to my own expectations instead of trying to please others. I am honest with myself about what I want and what I can achieve. I strive to be authentic.

I believe in myself and my abilities. I challenge doubts and assumptions that make me underestimate my potential. I reflect on my accomplishments. Each experience proves that I am capable and talented.

I team up with others. I find partners who share my vision.

I tolerate discomfort. I am willing to adjust my lifestyle and make tradeoffs that bring me closer to reaching my goals. Although I will change or do things differently to remove discomfort if it means I can still reach my goals. I do not have to live in discomfort to pay for my goals.

I take concrete action. I translate my dreams into specific steps and timelines. I make progress each day.

I choose happiness. I adopt habits that bring me satisfaction and success. I enjoy the journey. I am content with what I have while I continue to learn and grow.

Today, I connect with my highest ambitions and deepest desires. I am living out my dreams.

Self-Reflection

What do my dreams say about me and my values?

_____
_____
_____
_____

How can I make my dreams more practical?

_____
_____
_____
_____

What holds me back from following my dreams?

_____
_____
_____
_____

I Embrace Growth

I embrace growth.

I become stronger and wiser each day.

I make my wellbeing a top priority. I build a solid foundation for my personal development by taking care of my mental and physical health. I watch what I eat. I exercise regularly. I manage daily stress and sleep well at night.

I continue learning. I use my library card. I read books, watch videos, and listen to podcasts. I take courses online or at my local community college. I talk with friends and my team about their hobbies and interests.

I connect with others. I cultivate mutually supportive relationships. I share constructive feedback. I engage in deep discussions and listen carefully to different points of view.

I give generously. Practicing random acts of kindness increases my capacity for love.

I advance my career. I study thought leaders and high performers. I adapt their habits to suit my own style. I work on my communication and writing skills. I manage my time and maintain balance.

I seek out inspiration. I spend time outdoors. Natural beauty energises me and stimulates my creativity. I practice my faith. Prayer and reflection encourage my self-awareness. My life feels more joyful and meaningful.

I celebrate the power of positivity. I believe in myself and my abilities. I learn from experience. I give myself sincere compliments and invigorating pep talks.

Today, I am like a garden in full bloom. I flourish and thrive. I grow my talents with dedication, hard work, and perseverance.

Self-Reflection

Why is personal development a lifelong process?

_____
_____
_____
_____

What is my personal mission statement?

_____
_____
_____
_____

How do challenges help me to grow?

_____
_____
_____
_____

I Celebrate Both Small and Large Achievements

I celebrate both small and large achievements.

Winning comes in various shapes and forms. Even small achievements add up to a beautiful picture of progress.

My small wins come in the form of daily tasks successfully executed. I know the challenges that come with tackling the big picture of my various roles. It feels good to be able to break down that picture and churn through its smaller parts.

When I am at work, I ignore the noise of blaring deadlines. I maintain composure by breaking down the goals that go into hitting that mark.

The victory at the end of each project is sweeter when it is made up of small achievements. I encourage myself when I hit those. It keeps me from becoming frazzled. Slow and steady always wins the race.

Successfully repaying debt is a personal accomplishment that is cause for celebration. I see my increasing net worth as something to be proud of.

Progress is my target in both professional and personal areas of life. The progress of others is hardly relevant to me. I make myself my only competition. It is enough of a challenge to beat my own personal best at anything.

Today, my thoughts turn to my accomplishments for the hours behind me. I smile with pride when I use my time productively. Each day has its own wins, and it gives me pleasure to acknowledge each of them.

Self-Reflection

How do I keep myself from becoming unreasonably competitive?

_____
_____
_____
_____

How do I reward myself when I achieve bigger goals?

_____
_____
_____
_____

What effect does celebrating my achievements have on my will to persevere?

_____
_____
_____
_____

I Rewire My Brain

I rewire my brain.

I am taking measures to weed out old programs and install new, more efficient programming. I am the programmer of my brain.

The more I read about how powerful my beliefs are in programming my life, the more I pay attention to my beliefs. I sort out the old beliefs from my childhood and upgrade them to my adulthood.

I become acutely aware of my thoughts. I recognize that my thoughts come from my programming, and I catch those thoughts that no longer serve my highest good. I follow the stream back to the headwaters and purify the source of that old belief.

I ensure that I am only inputting useful information into my brain.

I am mindful of what podcasts I listen to. I am aware of what television programs I am programming into my brain. I pay attention to radio input. I pay attention to what music is playing in the background.

I expand my ability to be aware of all the information that is streaming into my head.

I deprogram people from my life that fail to enrich me in some way. I am also very aware of when it is appropriate to enrich other people's lives.

Today, I see with great clarity which thoughts, beliefs, and other input are useful and which ones negatively impact me. I reject the ones that fail to support my desired programming, leaving me with new-found positivity and confidence.

Self-Reflection

What old programs in my brain need to be eliminated?

_____
_____
_____
_____

What new programs am I ready to install?

_____
_____
_____
_____

What upgrades do I need to make in my life?

_____
_____
_____
_____

I Unlock My Potential

I unlock my potential.

Fulfilling my potential creates more meaning and happiness in my life. Each day brings me many ways to develop my potential.

I tackle challenging projects. I gain new knowledge and stretch my skills. I accept discomfort. I am willing to work hard and delay gratification. The time I spend learning a foreign language or playing the piano is more rewarding than watching television or talking on the phone for hours.

I persevere through obstacles and delays. I plan for possible setbacks and develop alternative solutions.

I build my confidence. I strengthen my belief in my abilities. I review my accomplishments and celebrate my victories. I analyze my personal strengths and how to leverage them.

I rely upon my faith. Through prayer and meditation, I understand the value and importance of my life. I appreciate my blessings. I feel ready and eager to use them wisely.

I seek out the company of those who inspire me to aim higher. I surround myself with family and friends who encourage and support me. I reflect on characters in books and figures in the news who have qualities and accomplishments that I admire.

I take care of myself. I eat nutritious foods, exercise daily, and manage stress. By protecting my wellbeing and establishing a sense of security, I create a strong foundation that helps me to pursue my goals.

Today, I strive to reach my full potential. I maximize the amazing powers that dwell within me.

Self-Reflection

What is one example of how I discovered a hidden strength?

_____
_____
_____
_____

How do I feel when someone recognizes my potential?

_____
_____
_____
_____

What are 3 words that I associate with activating my potential?

_____
_____
_____
_____

I Take Charge of My Destiny

I take charge of my destiny.

I gather the strength to overcome my obstacles. I am in charge of my life!

I release any thoughts that deter me from my destiny. I release the shackles of my past self-sabotaging thoughts. I throw off the moorings that have kept me in the harbour of old beliefs and set sail for my highest destiny.

I feel a newfound strength welling up inside me. I have cast off the old ways of my life. I am on my way to my best life ever!

I free myself of negative emotions. I fill the sails of my ship with inspiration. I am sailing into my future with confidence.

I boldly go where I have never gone before. I see my life as an adventure. I take charge of the wheel of fate!

I launch my life in a new direction! I see through the spyglass my ultimate future! I stay on course.

I navigate through life's challenges like a pro. I use my inner compass to guide my way. I allow the wind to fill my sails and keep sailing forward.

I make an immediate course correction when distractions do their best to throw me off. I feel confident that nothing can deter me from my goal.

Today, even when the winds of change come towards me, I have my hands firmly gripping the helm. I feel the wind at my back. I confidently sail into my future and ride the seas of time with grace and ease.

Self-Reflection

How can I gain more confidence in myself?

_____
_____
_____
_____

How can I overcome any doubt?

_____
_____
_____
_____

How can I feel like I am navigating my life like a ship captain?

_____
_____
_____
_____

I Produce Results

I produce results.

I am competent and capable. I meet my goals and deliver results.

I determine my priorities. I devote my time and energy to the activities that are meaningful to me. I block out time for my most important tasks when I arrange my weekly schedule.

I do one thing at a time. Being mindful helps me to reduce stress and accomplish more. I turn off my phone when I am eating dinner with my family. I pay attention to my body instead of watching TV news while I work out.

I stay organised. I create systems that help me to operate efficiently.

I take breaks regularly. I give myself time to relax and recharge. I take a walk around the block in between business meetings. I stop to play ball with my children when I am doing household chores.

I ask for feedback. I depend on others for input and advice so I can work smarter. I thank them for their time and let them know how their efforts have helped me.

I collaborate with others. Working as a team makes challenging projects more fun and successful. I discover new methods and ideas. I enjoy contributing my talents and sharing group victories.

I build my motivation. I stay on track by taking care of my health and remembering the purpose behind my tasks. I value each experience as an opportunity to learn and grow.

Today, I focus on being productive rather than being busy. I persevere until I get the results I want.

Self-Reflection

What is one positive habit that would help me to be more productive?

_____
_____
_____
_____

How can I minimise distractions at work?

_____
_____
_____
_____

How can small changes create big results?

_____
_____
_____
_____

I PRODUCE RESULTS

Travelling Inspires Me To Experience More

Travelling inspires me to experience more.

When the world feels small, I travel. I enjoy experiencing the enormous domain beyond my work and home. Sometimes, I escape to places far away. But I know that I can also drive down the road, or just beyond the city limits, to partake in the traveller's experience.

The world is vast, and I am aware that I am familiar with only a small part of it.

Encountering new cultures is an exciting experience. I enjoy meeting new people and observing different systems of society. Architecture, music, and food are fun areas of exploration.

Closer to home, I explore the great outdoors. I find hiking paths, lakes, and many other areas to visit. I take in my surroundings, enjoying both sight and sound. Leaving the stresses of work behind is necessary, because I want to keep my mind right here, in the moment.

I love traveling with others. My family enjoys the adventure as much as I do. I like sharing the experiences and discussing our discoveries.

Regardless of where I go, each time I travel, I expand my world.

Today, I intend to create travel plans for this weekend. By using my resources, I can locate sites and recreational areas that I have yet to visit. I am looking forward to my next great adventure!

Self-Reflection

What are my favourite recreational activities?

_____
_____
_____
_____

What benefits can I receive from experiencing other cultures?

_____
_____
_____
_____

Would I ever consider traveling alone? What are the pros and cons for me?

_____
_____
_____
_____

TRAVELLING Inspires Me TO Experience MORE

I Listen to my Heart

I listen to my heart.

My heart drives decisions that are tied to emotion. I know that deciding with emotion sometimes results in undesirable outcomes. But I give my heart great credit for keeping me connected with the softer side of people.

I rely on my heart to tell me when I am making the right choices for my happiness. I am careful with my definition of true happiness. I know I can rely on my heart to help me find it.

My family and friends are special to me. I like to make them happy by my words and actions.

I am also very honest with them. They deserve to know the sometimes undesirable realities of life. But at times, their emotional well-being takes precedence. I often find it necessary to overlook practical decisions to keep them happy.

Listening to my heart helps me be sympathetic with people in pain. Even when I am personally unaffected by an incident, I avoid appearing disconnected.

Emotional maturity means I am able to empathise when others need my support. I am careful to listen to their cues and do my best to cater to their emotional desires. My family members have a shoulder to lean on when their heart is aching.

Today, I am committed to achieving balance between emotional and practical thinking. Such equilibrium helps me to effectively handle situations. It also helps me to remain connected to those I care about.

Self-Reflection

In what scenarios does my heart unwisely cloud my judgment?

_____
_____
_____
_____

What is the best mental state to be in before making a decision tied to emotion?

_____
_____
_____
_____

How helpful is dialogue in helping others make wise decisions?

_____
_____
_____
_____

I Say Yes to Opportunities of a Lifetime

I say "yes" to opportunities of a lifetime.

Few things make me shriek with excitement. However, when fantastic opportunities come along, I embrace them with an open mind and wide-open arms.

Moving to the middle of Europe is a childhood dream come true. My stomach tingles with excitement because I know that I am about to experience wonder and joy. Although I only have a partial plan, that is enough for me to get up and go.

Being able to travel and work satisfies both personal and professional goals. There is a chance that this is a short-term opportunity, but I am still ready for it.

I now approach life with fearlessness. It feels so freeing to just say "yes" to things that are scary and uncertain. But my gut is my guide. Once it feels right to my insides, I know that solutions are bound to unfold.

When I say "yes" to rock climbing, I am confronting my fears. I refuse to continue living in fear of anything. My soul is open to transformation.

Although I feel the adrenaline rush that comes with doing something scary, I keep going. The higher I go, the more exhilarating the experience is.

I know that I am being filled by the sheer satisfaction of conquering a longstanding fear.

Today, I relish the feeling of freedom I get when I agree with my instincts and go after amazing opportunities. It is thrilling to unearth the host of emotions that I experience as I resist the urge to shy away and embrace the desire to live life to the fullest.

Self-Reflection

What are some of the things on my wish list that I am ready to do?

_____
_____
_____
_____

How much consideration do I give to my loved ones when I make big decisions?

_____
_____
_____
_____

How do I know when something is right for me?

_____
_____
_____
_____

I Am Honest with Myself

I am honest with myself.

I owe myself the truth.

I accept myself as I am. I understand my strengths and the areas where I need to grow. I pay attention to my feelings. I treat myself with kindness and respect.

I explore my motives. I think before I speak. I ask myself if what I have to say is accurate and helpful.

I stand up for my principles. I voice my concerns and take action. I remain calm. I respect others while following my own conscience.

I take responsibility for my actions. I hold myself accountable for my decisions. I focus on what I can control.

I face facts and consider other viewpoints, even when they challenge my beliefs and desires. I am optimistic and realistic. Acknowledging the full picture helps me to overcome obstacles and adapt to change.

I apologize when I disappoint myself or others. I express sincere regrets. I learn from the experience. I forgive myself and move forward.

I simplify my life and reduce daily stress. I strive to meet my own standards instead of conforming to external expectations. I rely on my own judgement rather than seeking approval from others.

I enjoy inner peace and contentment. I am comfortable with who I am.

Today, I am true to myself. I have the wisdom and courage to lead an authentic life. Being honest with myself enables me to learn and grow. My life becomes more meaningful and fulfilling.

Self-Reflection

How can I tell when I am being honest with myself?

_____
_____
_____
_____

How does being honest with myself affect my relationships with others?

_____
_____
_____
_____

What do I see when I look in the mirror?

_____
_____
_____
_____

I am Honest with Myself

Thank You!

Thank you for choosing this book and supporting my mission to make the world a more conscious place.

Please feel free to send me an email and let me know any ideas you have for more books you would like to see me produce, or if you have feedback on this book, I'd also be grateful to receive that. I try to respond to as many as emails as I can, but I don't have time to respond to every single one.

serenity@elyseburns-hill.com

Printed in Great Britain
by Amazon

35131727R00066